The United States

New Mexico

Paul Joseph
ABDO & Daughters

visit us at
www.abdopub.com

Published by Abdo & Daughters, 4940 Viking Drive, Suite 622, Edina, Minnesota 55435.
Copyright © 1998 by Abdo Consulting Group, Inc., Pentagon Tower, P.O. Box 36036,
Minneapolis, Minnesota 55435 USA. International copyrights reserved in all countries.
No part of this book may be reproduced in any form without written permission from the
publisher.

Printed in the United States.

Cover and Interior Photo credits: Peter Arnold, Inc., Superstock, Archive, Corbis-
Bettmann

Edited by Lori Kinstad Pupeza
Contributing editor Brooke Henderson
Special thanks to our Checkerboard Kids—Laura Jones, Jack Ward, Francesca Tuminelly

All statistics taken from the 1990 census; The Rand McNally Discovery Atlas of The
United States.

Library of Congress Cataloging-in-Publication Data

Joseph, Paul, 1970-
     New Mexico / Paul Joseph.
     p. cm. -- (United States)
     Includes index.
     Summary: Surveys the people, geography, and history of the state known as the
"Land of Enchantment."
     ISBN 1-56239-868-7
     1. New Mexico--Juvenile literature. [1. New Mexico.] I. Title. II. Series:
United States (series)
     F796.3.J67   1998
     978.9--dc21   97-16749
                                           CIP
                                           AC

Contents

Welcome to New Mexico

New Mexico is called the Land of Enchantment. It is usually very sunny and warm. The state has many scenic areas that attract thousands of visitors.

New Mexico's land is very open. It is filled with beautiful deserts and mountains. There are also incredible natural wonders in the state. There is Carlsbad Caverns National Park and White Sands National Monument to name two.

The area of New Mexico is very large. It is the fifth biggest state in the country. However, not many people live there. It ranks 37th in **population**. This makes for a lot of open land with few people.

The Land of Enchantment is a scenic highland of towering mountains, red rocks, and barren deserts. Along with the beautiful land are **Native American** villages,

Spanish mission houses, and the remains of ancient cliff dwellers.

The state is a mix of both old and new. Although New Mexico is one of the youngest states, it is the site of the oldest white **settlement** in the western United States.

Upper Dog Canyon, New Mexico.

Fast Facts

NEW MEXICO

Capital
Santa Fe (55,859 people)
Area
121,336 square miles
(314,259 sq km)
Population
1,521,779 people
Rank: 37th
Statehood
January 6, 1912
(47th state admitted)
Principal rivers
Rio Grande
Pecos River
Highest point
Wheeler Peak;
13,161 feet (4,011 m)
Largest city
Albuquerque (384,736 people)
Motto
Crescit eundo
(It grows as it goes)
Song
"Asi es Nuevo Mexico" and "O,
Fair New Mexico"
Famous People
Kit Carson, Georgia O'Keefe,
Jean Baptiste Lamy

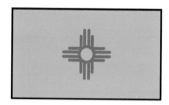

*S*tate Flag

*Y*ucca

*R*oadrunner

*P*inon

About New Mexico

The Land of Enchantment

Detail area

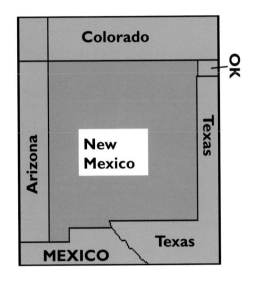

New Mexico's
abbreviation

Borders: west (Arizona), north (Colorado), east (Oklahoma, Texas), south (Texas, Mexico)

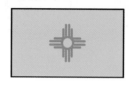

Nature's Treasures

The biggest treasure in the land of Enchantment is its beautiful land, which is a mixture of towering mountains and barren deserts.

The climate of New Mexico is also a wonderful treasure. The state has mostly dry weather. The people and visitors of New Mexico find it an especially healthful state because of the dry weather and lots of sunshine.

The Land of Enchantment is rich in **minerals**. The state is filled with petroleum, potassium salts, copper, and uranium. The open land in New Mexico is a treasure to the **cattle** and sheep that **graze**.

There are mountain ranges and valleys in New Mexico. Deserts that contain white sands cover the land. Wonderful lakes and the Rio Grande River flowing through the middle of the state are just a few of nature's treasures in New Mexico.

Rio Grande Gorge, Taos County, New Mexico.

Beginnings

Ancient pueblo ruins and cliff dwellings show that people lived there long before Europeans came to America. The first known people to live in New Mexico were **Native Americans**. Some of them were called the Acoma, Pueblo, Apache, and Navajo.

The first European to visit the state was the Spaniard Alvar Nunez Cabeza de Vaca in 1536. Juan de Onate arrived from Mexico with 400 people in 1598, and started a **settlement**.

Pedro de Peralta **founded** the city of Santa Fe in 1610, and made it the capital. The Pueblos did not like that the Spaniards were taking their land, so they fought back. In the revolt of 1680, they burned Santa Fe to the ground.

Twelve years later, the Spaniards took over again. They were in control until 1821 after Mexico took over the area. In 1828, **borders** between the United States and

Mexico were made. In 1848, New Mexico became part of the United States as part of the Treaty of Guadalupe Hidalgo.

In 1901, Jim White, a cowboy, discovered the Carlsbad Caverns in New Mexico. The area was set aside as a national monument in 1930. In 1912, New Mexico became the 47th state.

Pueblo dwelling, Taos, New Mexico.

B.C. to 1600

First People and First Explorers
Millions of years ago much of New Mexico was covered in water. Dinosaurs roamed the area.

Many years later the area was a dry region with mountains and deserts. **Native Americans** lived in the area. Some of the earliest tribes called themselves the Acoma, Pueblo, and Navajo.

1536: Cabeza de Vaca enters New Mexico from Texas.

1539: Marcos de Niza **explores** New Mexico and claims the area for Spain.

1598: Juan de Onate claims New Mexico for Spain, and sets up a **settlement**.

New Mexico

B.C. to 1600

1600 to 1900

New Cities and New Owners

 1610: Pedro do Peralta, **governor** of New Mexico, **founds** Santa Fe and moves the state capital there.

 1706: Albuquerque is founded.

 1821: Mexico wins independence from Spain and takes over New Mexico.

 1848: After a war between Mexico and the United States, Mexico gives up New Mexico and California to the United States.

 1850: The United States Territory of New Mexico is created.

New Mexico

1600 to 1900

1900s

Statehood and Beyond

 1912: New Mexico becomes the 47th state on January 6.

 1933: Carlsbad Caverns National Park is created.

 1962: Navajo Dam on San Juan River is completed.

 1974: Jerry Apodaca becomes the first Spanish American elected as **governor** since 1918.

 1988: Severe drought destroys part of the state. Wind erosion damages more than 1.4 million acres of land.

New Mexico

1900s

New Mexico's People

There are about 1.5 million people living in the state of New Mexico. The first known people to live in the area were **Native Americans**. There were the Mogollon, Anasazi, Navajo, and Apache.

New Mexico has had many famous people come from its state. Conrad Hilton was born in San Antonio, New Mexico. He bought his first hotel in 1918. In 1946, he formed the Hilton Hotels Corporation. Today, Hilton Hotels are all over the world.

Billy the Kid lived in New Mexico from the 1870s until his death in 1881. He was actually famous for being an outlaw, thief, and murderer. He was the leader of one of the most well-known group of outlaws.

Dennis Chavez was born and raised in New Mexico. He was the state's **representative** from 1931 to 1935.

From 1935 to 1962 he was New Mexico's **senator**. He was well-known for his work and support of fair wages, benefits, and safety for workers.

Other famous people are authors Mary Austin and Ann Nolan Clark. John Lewis was a famous jazz musician. Al Unser, Sr., Al Unser, Jr., and Bobby Unser are the greatest auto racing family of all-time.

Dennis Chavez

Bobby Unser

Billy the Kid

Desert Cities

The state of New Mexico does not have many large cities. Only one city, Albuquerque, has more than 100,000 people.

Albuquerque is on the Rio Grande River near the center of the state. Many people visit this wonderful city for its great weather and many things to do. There are museums, theaters, and sporting events. Also the University of New Mexico is located here.

Las Cruces is the second largest city in the state with over 60,000 people. It is located near the southern **border**, very close to Texas. This city is a beautiful farming area. It is also home to New Mexico State University.

Santa Fe is the capital and the third largest city. It was **founded** in 1610 by the

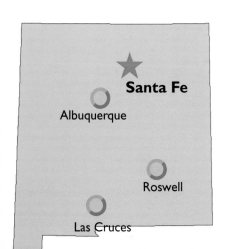

Spanish. There are many **tourist resorts** along with museums, old churches, and historic monuments.

Roswell, where Bottomless Lakes State Park is, and Hobbs, the oil capital of the state, are two other cities in New Mexico.

Albuquerque, New Mexico

New Mexico's Land

New Mexico's land is mostly mountainous. Mountain peaks can be seen from every part of the state except in the very southeast. The Land of Enchantment has four different regions.

The Rocky Mountain Region enters New Mexico from Colorado. It is in the middle north and reaches south about 120 miles (193 km) in a chain of peaks. The Rockies are split by the Rio Grande River. This region also has Wheeler Peak—the highest point in the state at 13,161 feet (4,011 m).

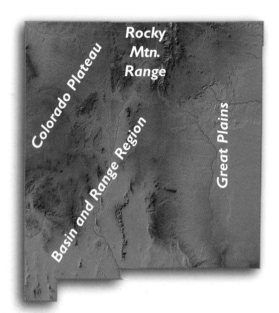

The Colorado Plateau Region is in the northwest corner of the state. It is a region of flat-topped hills that rise straight up from the

22

plains. The most famous hill is called Acoma Rock. Other features of this region are the San Juan Valley and the Zuni Mountains.

The Basin and Range Region covers most of the middle and the entire southwest part of the state. There are several mountain ranges along with many salt flats and white sand dunes. The Rio Grande flows through this region. East of the river is the White Sands National Monument.

The Great Plains Region covers the entire eastern side of the state. The southern part of this region is called the Llano Estacado (Staked Plain). Close to the Texas **border** in the south is Carlsbad Caverns National Park. Nearby is the lowest point in the state. It is Red Bluff Reservoir at 2,817 feet (859 m).

White Sands, National Monument, New Mexico.

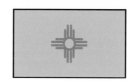

New Mexico at Play

New Mexico is a great place to play because of the weather, land, and many things to do. The people who live in the state and the many visitors enjoy playing in the Land of Enchantment.

A major attraction to New Mexico is the Carlsbad Caverns National Park. This park has the largest known underground chambers. The Big Room in the park has a 200 foot (61 m) ceiling, 14 acres of floor space, and is more than 800 feet (244 m) underground. It is truly an awesome sight.

Because of the dry, sunny weather, people golf on courses with mountain and desert views. People can swim and boat in the lakes. In the winter, New Mexico's mountains offer some of the best skiing in the land.

The state also has nine national monuments, seven national forests, and many state parks. There are also more than 40 dude ranches and other **resorts** for **tourists**.

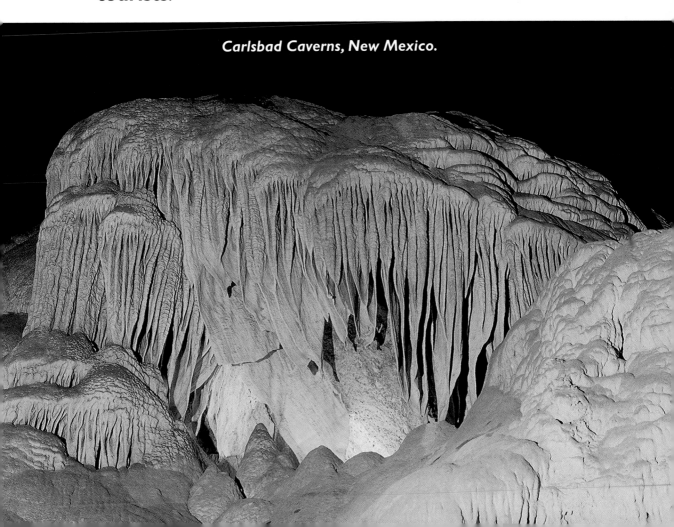

Carlsbad Caverns, New Mexico.

New Mexico at Work

The people of New Mexico must work to make money. Serving out-of-state vacationers and **tourists** is one of the biggest jobs in the state.

Because of all the **tourism** in New Mexico, there are lots of service jobs there. Service is cooking and serving food, working in **resorts**, hotels, restaurants, stores, and banks.

Farming is another source of income for people. The sale of **cattle** makes the most money in **agriculture**. Milk, sheep, lambs, and wool bring in a lot of money for New Mexico farmers, too. They also grow hay, barley, corn, and pecans.

Mining is another big business in New Mexico. **Minerals** bring in nearly six billion dollars a year. But making electrical things is the biggest business of all in New Mexico.

There are so many different things to do in the Land of Enchantment. It is no wonder that many people visit it each year. Because of the beauty, weather, people, land, mountains, and rivers, New Mexico is a great place to visit, live, work, and play.

A cattle round-up in Chama, New Mexico.

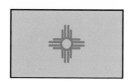

Fun Facts

•New Mexico is shaped roughly like a rectangle. At the northwest corner of the state is the only point in the nation where four states meet—New Mexico, Colorado, Arizona, and Utah. At that area a person can be in four different states in a matter of minutes!

•Santa Fe was named the capital of New Mexico in 1610. Almost 400 years later it is still the capital of the state.

•Today, New Mexico is a blend of three cultures—**Native Americans**, Mexican-American, and American. It is the only state with two official languages—English and Spanish.

•The highest point in New Mexico is Wheeler Peak. It is 13,161 feet (4,011 m) tall. The lowest area is Red Bluff Reservoir. It is 2,817 feet (859 m).

•New Mexico is the fifth largest state. Its land covers 121,336 square miles (314,259 sq km).

A Navajo girl in New Mexico.

Glossary

Agriculture: another name for farming.

Border: neighboring states, countries, or waters; to be along side something.

Cattle: farm animals such as cows, bulls, and oxen.

Explorers: people who explore places where not many people have been before.

Found: started, began.

Governor: the highest elected official in the state.

Graze: animals eating grass.

Minerals: things found in the earth, such as rock, diamonds, or coal.

Miners: people who work underground to get minerals.

Mining: digging underground to get minerals.

Native Americans: the first people who were born and lived in North America.

Population: the number of people living in a certain place.

Representative: a person who is elected by the people to represent a certain area. He or she goes to Washington, D.C., makes laws, and is part of the House of Representatives.

Resort: a place to vacation that has fun things to do.

Senator: one of two elected officials from a state that represents the state in Washington, D.C. There, he or she makes laws and is a part of Congress.

Settlement: a place or region that a group of people have moved to.

Tourism: an industry that serves people who are traveling for fun, and visiting places of interest.

Tourists: people who travel for fun.

Internet Sites

New Mexico Land of Sun and Chile
http://www-psych.nmsu.edu/~linda/chilepg.htm

This website has a lot to offer. It has everything having to do with New Mexico with tons of links and fun trivia. Everything from magazines and media, to tourism, museums and libraries, to big events, and more.

This site is subject to change. Go to your favorite search engine and type in New Mexico for more sites.

PASS IT ON

Tell Others Something Special About Your State
To educate readers around the country, pass on interesting tips, places to see, history, and little unknown facts about the state you live in. We want to hear from you!
To get posted on ABDO & Daughters website, e-mail us at "mystate@abdopub.com"

Index